# Hand Embroidered Country Scenes

## Lazy summer days

LEILA SUTCLIFFE
*See Page 1*

*This embroidery is worked in multi-shaded threads which have been dyed by Leila. French knots are scattered over long and short background stitches in the background. The chair is made from fine wood which was purchased from a model shop and then washed with white paint. The hat is made from builders' scrim which was dipped into fabric stiffener and moulded over a thimble. In the foreground Leila uses a variety of threads which are stiffened with fabric stiffener. Poppies are attached to some of the threads and the daisies are worked on cold water soluble fabric.*

*115 x 150mm (4¹/₂ x 5⁷/₈in)*

## 'Twas on a Monday morning

JUDITH MASON
*See opposite*

*Long and short stitches are worked in front of the French knot trees to create a wall. The herbaceous border is made up of lazy daisy stitch and French knots, and the three-dimensional flowers are all worked on cold water soluble fabric. The washing line is held up by a small piece of wood, and the clothes are small rectangles of coloured habotai silk. Needleweaving is used to create the washing basket and Judith painstakingly made the six tiny pegs.*

*195 x 115mm (7⁵/₈ x 4¹/₂in)*

# Hand Embroidered Country Scenes

## Sue Newhouse

SEARCH PRESS

First published in Great Britain 1997

Search Press Limited
Wellwood, North Farm Road,
Tunbridge Wells, Kent TN2 3DR

Text copyright © Sue Newhouse
Photographs by Search Press Studios
with the exception of the photograph of Scruffy on page 44

ISBN 0 85532 819 3 (PB)
ISBN 0 85532 829 0 (C)

*Suppliers*
If you have any difficulty in obtaining any of the materials and
equipment mentioned in this book, then please write for a
current list of stockists, including firms who operate a mail-order
service, to the Publishers.
Search Press Limited, Wellwood,
North Farm Road, Tunbridge Wells,
Kent TN2 3DR, England

*Acknowledgements*
The author would like to thank her mother, Dorothy Howorth
for helping her to type and check the manuscript; Hee Bee
Designs of Willow Green, Cheshire; Mrs G M Parker of the
Patchwork Gallery, Knutsford; Leila Sutcliffe of Chelford,
Cheshire; Jacqueline and Michael Hyman of the Textile
Restoration Studio, Altringham, for the loan of all their
equipment on pages 8–11. Most of all she would like to thank
her students who generously allowed her to use their
embroideries, without which the book would not have been
possible. Her sincere apologies are extended to all those whose
work has not been included due to lack of space, even though this
book is longer than the last one!

Printed in Spain by Elkar S. Coop. Bilbao 48012

*Bluebells in the mist*
REBECCA SCHOFIELD

Rebecca has stitched the grass background, couched
down a hessian tree, then covered the embroidery
with chiffon. More bluebells, grass and trees are
added, and covered with another layer of chiffon.
Finally, the foreground tree and bluebells are added.
She has achieved a feeling of distance and a misty
atmosphere by using the chiffon.
50 x 150mm (2 x 5⁷/₈in)

# Contents

# Introduction

Since my first book *Creative Hand Embroidery* was published, my students' work has become more innovative and fascinating. They are producing inspirational embroideries, and gaining a lot more confidence with every piece they produce. Skills are being passed on to new students and fresh ideas are constantly being created as we explore landscapes, flowers and gardens.

Every year, old and new students meet during the September enrolments. Their first project takes them through all the techniques and stitches, and I usually start them off with a simple meadow. The second project is either a cornfield or a woodland scene, or, if they prefer, it could be a flower border. By the time January arrives, new confidences and skills have been gained and slowly fresh ideas and talents emerge.

In May I open my house to the students and we spend an enjoyable five days together, stitching and discussing the landscapes, trees, flowers and grasses that are being embroidered. Most of us are avid gardeners, and there is a constant exchange of knowledge during this time. Even if we cannot remember the name of a plant, we can recall how it looks and we are able to reproduce it in fabric and thread. Observation is important, and I help the students when they have difficulties, showing them the big-leafed plants near my pond, or the maroon-leafed plant beside my patio, encouraging them to use their newly acquired skills.

I start this book with a step-by-step sequence showing how to stitch a cornfield. Fabric poppies and ears of corn are applied over straight stitch and French knots, to add depth. The techniques are simple and you should be able to create your own landscape if you follow these instructions. A stitch sampler illustrates how, by changing the colour of the threads, a whole range of flowers can be embroidered. Then there is a section showing how to make fabric flowers, grasses and leaves. Further sections show how to create atmosphere, depth and perspective, how to use different fabrics and found objects, and how to mount and finish your pictures.

I have gathered together a range of work from my students and written the book for all those who are inspired by nature and the world around us, and for those who love working with fabric and thread. There is no right or wrong way of interpreting what you see. Try the techniques and you will see how easy it is. Learn how to recreate the beauty of the countryside.

## Rose Arch

### FIONA BATEMAN

*French knots and lazy daisy stitch decorate the border and straight stitch is used for the grass. The arch is made from fine wood. Painted silk roses and leaves decorate the arch and the hydrangeas are worked on cold water soluble fabric. The lavender is hand crocheted and attached to the fabric with tiny stitches.*

*180 x 225mm (7 x 9in)*

# Materials and equipment

I always recommend items that are simple, easy to obtain and economical. This page shows a selection of the items I use; they are not all illustrated. The following list should be treated as a guide only. You do not need all the items in order to produce good embroideries.

## MATERIALS

Good quality white cotton sheeting
White habotai silk
Cold water soluble fabric
Hessian
Silk crepeline
Chiffon
Stranded cotton or silk embroidery threads
Invisible threads
Black, yellow, blue, red poster paints
PVA conservation fabric stiffener
PVA adhesive
Mounting card
White self-hardening or oven-bakable modelling clay
Florist's wire

## EQUIPMENT

Two embroidery ring frames, 75–100mm (3–4in) and 200–220mm (8–8⅞in) diameter
The finest needle you can thread
Small, sharp scissors
White palette
6mm (¼in) square paintbrush
Water soluble or air soluble pen
Craft knife

## SILK THREADS

Silk threads are made in a variety of beautiful colours. They have a sheen and they are readily available, either twisted as shown here, or stranded. They are particularly suitable for this type of hand embroidery which is worked on painted silk, backed with white cotton sheeting.

Most scenes can be interpreted with a surprisingly small number of stitches, and with a range of threads. However, I prefer to use silk threads in a selected range of carefully chosen colours to reflect the tones and textures of the countryside. I always choose my colours in daylight. Electric light alters the colours and shades of the threads, so be careful when selecting the shades you need.

The threads can be used in several ways. They can be stitched on to the painted silk background in the normal way, or used to create three-dimensional flowers and grasses. The buttonhole bar method on page 22 shows how to create daisies, buttercups, poppies, bluebells, lavender and grass, by simply knotting the threads. A single strand of dark green stiffened thread is ideal for the tiny stems of the fabric flowers shown throughout the book.

Subtle uses of colour can create a feeling of depth, enrich landscapes, add a sparkle to dark corners and enhance brightly coloured scenes. French knots, lazy daisy stitch and bullion knots are ideal for different flower heads. The silk sheen adds a lustre to fields, borders and gardens. Straight stitch and fly stitch can be worked in any direction, and the silk threads are ideal for capturing fields of swaying grass with wooded borders. Embroidery is tactile and therefore the rich feel of the silk threads and the textured stitches add interest to an otherwise flat image.

*Silk threads in a range of carefully chosen colours.*

## HAND-DYED THREADS

With all the colours that are available, it is still sometimes difficult to find the exact shade you need when you are working on a particular group of flowers, a woodland scene, or a colourful garden. It is possible, with all the dyes available, to colour your own multi-shaded threads, similar to the threads shown opposite. Blues, greens, yellows and reds can all be enhanced by simply dyeing them. The colours can be subtly changed so that you could have shades of green with a splash of blue, for a bluebell wood; shades of mauves for lavender and wisteria; shades of warm brown for country gates and stone walls; and painted backgrounds can be complemented with chosen hues. Embroidery becomes more exciting when you can create your own colours.

## BINDING AN EMBROIDERY FRAME

It is important that the fabric is taut in the embroidery frame so that the threads can be stitched on to a firm background. If the fabric is not taut, the stitches will cause the background to distort, resulting in a badly finished embroidery. It is well worth taking some extra time to prepare your materials and to bind the frames securely.

A ring frame consists of one wooden ring fitted inside another, between which the fabric is tensioned, the stretched fabric surface uppermost. In order to prevent the fabric from slipping, it is a good idea to bind the inner ring with some white cotton sheeting. Simply tear a few lengths approximately 25mm (1in) wide, wind them around the ring, and secure the last one with a few stitches on the inside. When working on a very fine fabric, such as habotai silk, it is advisable to bind the outer ring as well.

*Multi-shaded silk threads
hand-dyed by Leila Sutcliffe.*

# Stitches

Approximately eight stitches are used to create all the embroideries illustrated in this book. A wonderful variety of flowers, grasses, trees and foliage can be embroidered by using a combination of the stitches shown, or by working the same stitch with different coloured threads. Some of these are shown on page 14. For example, daisies and sunflowers can be embroidered using lazy daisy stitch with white or yellow thread. More examples can be found throughout the book. Always study the flower, tree or plant you want to embroider before you start to stitch, and choose the appropriate stitches to interpret your scene.

Your work will be more enjoyable and exciting if you spend some time practising these stitches before you start. Use one strand of thread only and the finest needle that you can manage. Always stretch your fabric in an embroidery frame before starting to stitch, and check it frequently to ensure that it remains taut, otherwise your stitches will distort the image you are creating.

## STRAIGHT STITCH

This can be worked in any direction, in varying lengths, close together or wide apart.

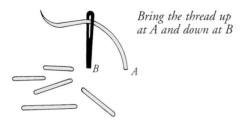

*Bring the thread up at A and down at B*

*Finish one stitch before starting the next one*

## SEEDING STITCH

Seeding stitches are tiny stitches of equal lengths worked randomly in all directions. They should appear as specks on the fabric, rather than short stitches.

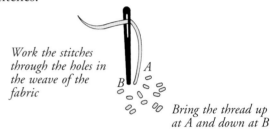

*Work the stitches through the holes in the weave of the fabric*

*Bring the thread up at A and down at B*

## TUFTING

Use six strands of thread and make a small straight stitch on the back of the fabric as shown.

*Take the thread down at A and up at B*

*Cut the threads on either side. The ideal length to leave is 12mm ($^1/_2$in) for each.*

## BLANKET STITCH

Work from left to right (or right to left if left-handed). To finish off, take the thread to the back of the fabric and secure it by working it into the stitches.

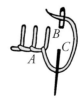

*Bring the thread up at A down at B and up at C*

*Bring the needle up over the thread to complete the stitch*

## LAZY DAISY STITCH

This is also known as detached chain stitch. When you have finished the stitch, either secure the thread at the back of the fabric for a single stitch, or bring it back to the front ready to work the next stitch.

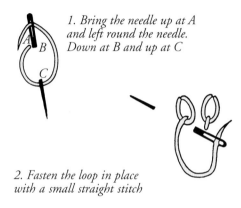

*1. Bring the needle up at A and left round the needle. Down at B and up at C*

*2. Fasten the loop in place with a small straight stitch*

## FLY STITCH

This stitch can be used singly, arranged in patterns, or worked in a line. The 'tail' can be lengthened, and the length and angle of the 'arms' can be varied.

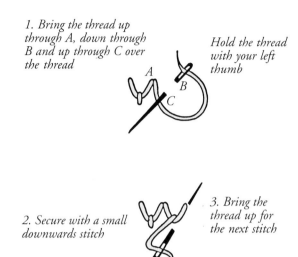

*1. Bring the thread up through A, down through B and up through C over the thread*

*Hold the thread with your left thumb*

*2. Secure with a small downwards stitch*

*3. Bring the thread up for the next stitch*

## FRENCH KNOT

Use one strand of thread. When the stitch has been completed, either secure the knot, or bring the thread up through the fabric to work the next knot.

*1. Bring the thread up at A. Hold the thread in your left hand and twist the needle once around it*

*2. Twist the needle back to the starting point and re-insert close to A*

## BULLION KNOT

Follow stages one, two and three. When the knot is complete, pull the thread through to the back of the fabric until it lies flat.

*1. Bring the thread up at A, down at B and up again at A*

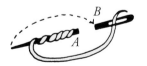

*2. Twist the thread around the needle and pull the needle through*

*3. Bring the needle back and re-insert it in A*

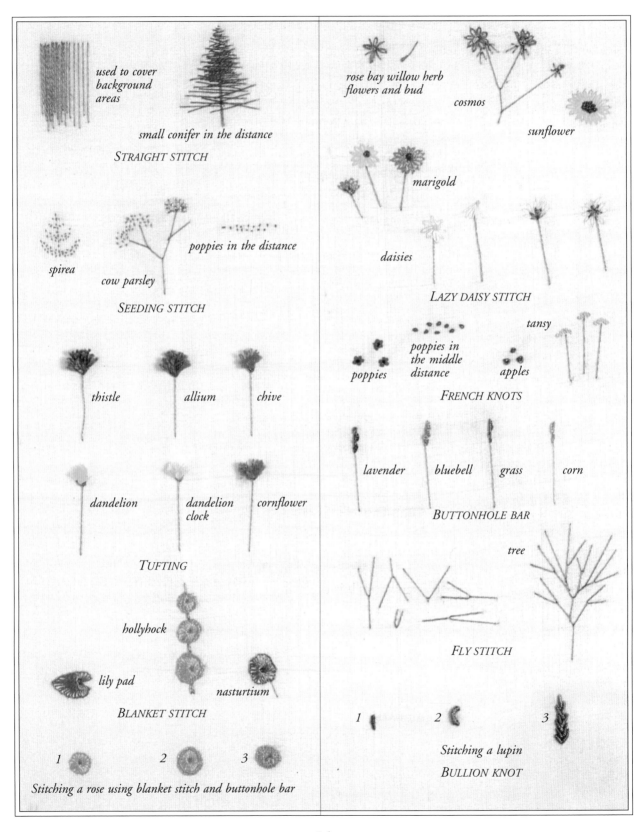

used to cover
background
areas

small conifer in the distance

STRAIGHT STITCH

rose bay willow herb
flowers and bud

cosmos

sunflower

marigold

spirea

poppies in the distance

cow parsley

daisies

SEEDING STITCH

LAZY DAISY STITCH

tansy

poppies in
the middle
distance

poppies

apples

thistle

allium

chive

FRENCH KNOTS

lavender

bluebell

grass

corn

dandelion

dandelion
clock

cornflower

BUTTONHOLE BAR

TUFTING

tree

hollyhock

FLY STITCH

lily pad

nasturtium

BLANKET STITCH

1                    2                    3

*1*          *2*          *3*

Stitching a lupin

*Stitching a rose using blanket stitch and buttonhole bar*

BULLION KNOT

## INTERPRETING THE COUNTRYSIDE

The eight stitches described on the pages 12 and 13 can be used in a variety of ways to interpret all aspects of the countryside. For example, straight stitch is ideal for filling in backgrounds, for gates and fences and for some fir trees. Distant flowers can be created by using one seeding stitch for each tiny bloom.

Tufting is wonderfully versatile. Here, one of my students has created a garlic wood using white threads tufted into the distinctive small white flowers of the garlic plant. They show up beautifully against the dark trees in the background. Tufts of variegated blue threads make realistic cornflowers, while long and short tufts of variegated greens can be used to create an impression of chaotic clumps of grass.

Lazy daisy stitch can be used in a variety of ways. It is extremely versatile. The daisies on pages 30 and 31 are worked in this stitch on cold water soluble fabric. The flowers are then cut out, attached to stiffened thread, and sewn on to the fabric background. Elsewhere in the book there are many examples of lazy daisy stitched flowers.

French knots are useful for filling in backgrounds. They give an impression of leaves in distant trees and bushes. I also use them for portraying flowers in fields and borders, or adding texture to walls.

Buttonhole bar (see page 22) is used to make a variety of different three-dimensional flowers, which are trimmed and attached to the embroideries with tiny stitches.

Fly stitch is useful for portraying distant trees. It is used effectively with groups of small French knots. The single threads can be stitched in different ways to give the impression of smaller and larger branches.

The sampler opposite shows the different ways you can interpret the stitches, and more ways are shown throughout the book. A variety of these stitches can also be used to represent one flower, depending upon its position in the landscape. For example, when creating poppies, red seeding can be used in the far distance, French knots in the middle distance and four to five French knots with one black knot in the

## Garlic Wood
### JENNY HEWINS

*Jenny has captured the cool, dappled light of a wood. French knots and long and short stitches are used on the distant background to imply dense foliage. Simple long and short stitches are used to cover the ground and seeding is used in the distance to give the impression of wild garlic. The foreground flowers are tufted and the painted silk leaves are stitched into the fabric.*

*100 x 145mm (4 x 5¾in)*

centre can be used in the foreground. If more detail is required you can make fabric poppies (see page 24).

The countryside can be interpreted in many ways. Be prepared to change your colours to suit your subject, and to experiment with different stitches.

# The Cornfield

This is an easy introduction to the basic techniques of stitching a landscape. The instructions are only a guide; if several people were to work on this embroidery, each picture would be different. For example, some may want to develop the foreground details; others may feel more interest is required in the distance or on the horizon line.

## MATERIALS

You do not need all the materials listed on page 9. Below are all the things you need to complete your first scene.

White habotai batik silk and white cotton sheeting, each 250 x 250mm (10 x 10in)

Threads: red to match the red poster paint for the poppies, three shades of corn colour for the field – pale, medium and slightly darker; pale and mid green

Poster paints, blue and red

Fabric stiffener

Mounting card

PVA adhesive

## EQUIPMENT

Two ring frames
Needle
Scissors
Palette
Small paint brush

## METHOD

Stretch the silk on to the bound ring frames. To do this separate the two rings and loosen the screw on the outer frame. Lay the silk over the inner ring. Press the outer ring over it pulling the fabric out gently until it is taut, keeping the grain straight. Tighten the screw carefully to secure the silk.

*Step 1*

Painting skies in a landscape gives it a realistic feel. A paler sky is probably better than a darker sky. To help you see the paint more clearly when you apply it to the silk, place a piece of white paper beneath the frame. Lightly wet the silk with water. Brush a pale blue wash across the fabric, working with the grain. If the silk starts to sag, pull it gently around the frame keeping the grain straight. If the blue is too dark, place the silk under running water. If it is too pale, wet the silk and add more blue. Dry the silk as quickly as you can with a hair-dryer to prevent water marks. When the silk is completely dry, take it off the frame.

Back the silk with white cotton sheeting; make sure the grain of the fabric is running in the same direction on each piece. Re-stretch both fabrics on to the frame. Cut a rectangle out of card 75 x 100mm (3 x 4in). Place it on the silk. Make sure the grain of the fabric is running in the same direction as the longest sides of the rectangle.

## Step 2

Using white thread tack around the template.

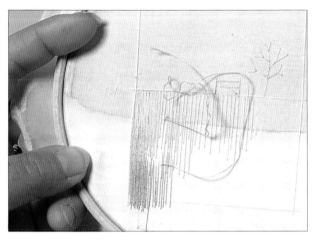

## Step 3

Tack a line to mark the horizon. Stitch the gate by working two upright stitches for the posts, 12mm (¹/₂in) apart. Using straight stitches, stitch horizontally across the top, middle and bottom of the gap. Work a stitch from the top left corner across to the bottom right corner. Using one strand of pale green, stitch the tree using fly stitch. With one strand of pale corn thread, work vertical straight stitch across the silk below the horizon line. Fill the gaps by working back and forth. Change the shade of your threads and work the second and third rows.

## Step 4

You now have a solid field of corn, starting with the pale corn colour at the top, graduating to a darker yellow at the base. Thread your needle with one strand of pale green thread and work the French knots for the hedge. Using a thread one shade darker, sprinkle small French knots over the tree adding seeding stitches around the edges of the clusters. Sprinkle French knots at the base of the hedge to create an interesting shadow, using a slightly darker shade of green.

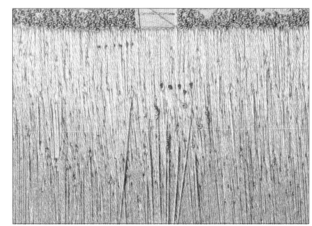

## Step 5

Thread your needle with one strand of red thread. Work some seeding stitches at the back of the field and French knots in the centre, to create an impression of poppy heads.

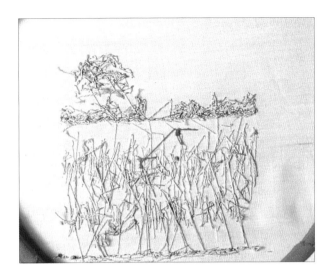

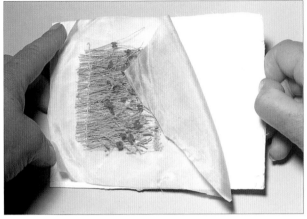

*Step 7*

The back of the embroidery will be covered with a tangle of stitches by now. Do not worry, this will all be covered up when your work is mounted! Work the ends of threads into existing stitches to secure them.

Trim the stems along the bottom. Remove the embroidery from the frame; trim the excess fabric leaving 37mm (1½in) around the image. Cut a piece of card the same size as the fabric. Place the fabric on the card and fold it back. Apply a 12mm (½in) line of glue to the card. Allow the cotton backing to fall on to the adhesive, which will stay wet for a few minutes; straighten the fabric by dragging it down with your fingers. Glue down the sides one at a time, making sure not to pull one side further over than the other. Keep the glue away from the embroidery. It will stain and you will not be able to remove it.

*Step 6*

To create a three-dimensional effect, add cornflowers, poppies and corn heads. These are made separately and attached to the bottom of the field with tiny stitches. The cornflowers are made by attaching little blue tufts to green thread. The poppies are made from painted silk (see page 24) and the corn is made using the hand crochet method (see page 36).

*Step 8*

Repeat the process with the silk. Keep stretching from left to right until it is glued down. At this stage it will have ripples in it running from the stitches into the sky. Simply turn your embroidery round and glue the bottom, then the two sides.

## *Cornfield*

### BRENDA HEWITT

*An example of the finished embroidery. Brenda has
decided to add small blue cornflowers to her
cornfield. They are made by attaching blue threads
to stiffened stems.*

*75 x 100mm (3 x 4in)*

# Three-dimensional flowers and foliage

Now you have completed a simple cornfield and learnt a few basic stitches, try creating your own scene. Before you start, it is important to know how flowers and foliage grow. Botanical knowledge is not essential, but you will find the subject is much easier to grasp if you are familiar with your garden or the countryside. Study your everyday surroundings and you will be amazed at the richness of colour and texture to be found in the most mundane of places.

Quiet corners and dark woodlands often reveal a bewildering variety of subject matter. Wild flowers and grasses nestle in urban roadsides, the central reservations of motorways, gardens, river banks, hillsides and fields. Flowers and foliage are abundant in gardens and parks. As the seasons change, these sites can look wonderful, particularly when they are coated with sparkling frost or gossamer cobwebs. Take time to notice how the plants relate to one another, in terms of colour, tone and texture.

In the Cornfield opposite, Leila Sutcliffe chose not to stitch a straight horizon with a hedge. Instead, she has flat stitched undulating hills. Small pieces of wood are tucked into the foreground, giving the impression of an old fence. Three-dimensional flowers and grasses are inserted around the fence, framing the picture and leading the viewer's eye inwards.

Distant details can be stitched, and interest can be created in the foreground by adding three-dimensional flowers and grasses. In this section I show you how to create foliage and flowers using paint, fabric and thread. The techniques are simple and extremely effective. A simple landscape can be transformed if you follow the instructions on the next few pages.

There are several ways to create three-dimensional flowers and foliage. The buttonhole bar method shown on page 22 is a simple technique using single strands of thread. With this method, a variety of tiny flowers and grasses can easily be made. Daisies become buttercups by changing the thread colour – and poppies become bluebells. These small flowers can be stitched on to the embroidery as shown in Carol Allan's embroidery on page 50.

Small silk flowers are used to decorate the majority of the embroideries shown in the book. They are made from small pieces of painted silk fabric (see page 24) which are attached to thread stems. It is Leila who introduced the stiffened threads as stems into the embroideries. That small step has helped to enhance the work of all my students. The method is used in many different ways and certainly adds a feeling of reality to all the landscapes.

Flowers can also be made using cold water soluble fabric (see pages 30, 40 and 43). If you can embroider a daisy, you will be able to stitch a rose bay willow herb by just changing your thread from white to pink. If you look at the embroidery opposite, rose bay willow herb is stitched into the picture on the left hand side.

## Cornfield
### LEILA SUTCLIFFE

*Leila dyes her own threads in a beautiful range of different shades, which she then uses on her embroideries. Here, the colours chosen reflect the beauty of the cornfield on a sunny day. Her range of threads is shown on the band along the base of the embroidery.*

*180 x 190mm (7 x 7¹/₂in)*

# *Thread flowers*

Flowers can be made easily, by working separate knots on to green threads.

## BUTTONHOLE BAR

Flowers, as well as grasses, can be made using this method. I find the best way to work is with the thread tied to two chair legs. Tie the thread tightly around the chair legs and secure each end with masking tape. Follow the method shown in the photograph. When you reach the end of the thread, go back to the beginning, stiffen and cut off the connecting threads, so that you are left with the stretched thread and the knot clusters. When it is dry, cut the thread into 25mm (1in) stems. You will be left with a bunch of stems topped with seed heads. The flowers below are made using this method. The knotted heads are made using different coloured threads.

*Tie a green thread between the legs of an upturned chair. Loop a second coloured thread around the stretched thread and pull it through. Work six tight loops, leave a gap of 25mm (1in); work six more tight loops. Continue until you reach the end of the stretched thread. Two or three loops will give a smaller flower; six or nine loops will give you a larger flower.*

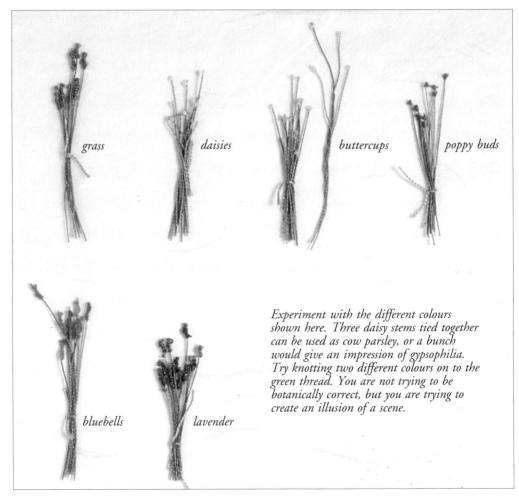

*grass*

*daisies*

*buttercups*

*poppy buds*

*bluebells*

*lavender*

*Experiment with the different colours shown here. Three daisy stems tied together can be used as cow parsley, or a bunch would give an impression of gypsophilia. Try knotting two different colours on to the green thread. You are not trying to be botanically correct, but you are trying to create an illusion of a scene.*

## Spring Picnic
### KATE MARTIN-BIRD

*Kate has covered the background with flat long and short stitches, using one strand of thread. The table cloth is a small piece of habotai silk; the pattern is drawn on to the fabric surface with felt tipped pens. The branches of the overhanging tree and the small hat are made out of hessian.*

*110 x 130mm (4³/₈ x 5¹/₈in)*

# Silk flowers

## SIMPLE METHOD

Here I show how to make a poppy. By simply paint-ing the silk fabric another colour, a wide variety of different flowers can be made. The embroideries on pages 25 and 50 show how realistic these little flowers can be.

To follow this method, first pour a little red poster paint into a palette. A field of poppies will require many flower heads, so cut out several long strips of white silk and dip them into the paint, stroking it on to the fabric with a small brush until the white of the fabric disappears. Allow the silk to dry completely. Do not leave it on a flat surface to dry, but instead, hang it up or speed up the process by drying it with a hair-dryer. Brush diluted fabric stiffener on to the silk and hang it up to dry. If you do not do this, the fabric will dry with a shine.

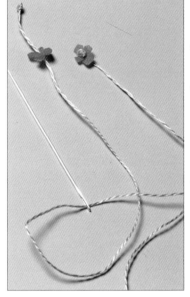

*Pull the needle through the poppy until it rests by the knot, which now forms the flower centre. Cut the stem and stiffen the whole flower with fabric stiffener, then hang upside down to dry. The flowers can be attached to your embroidery either singly or in bunches, as shown in the Cornfield (see page 18). Attach them to the fabric background using small running stitches along the bottom of the stems.*

*Using sharp scissors, cut as many small circles as you need from the painted and stiffened silk.*

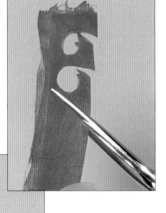

*Place one fabric circle on to a needle which has been threaded with a single strand of knotted pale green thread. Cut V-shapes into the circle and cut off the points.*

## POLYSTYRENE METHOD

Roses can be shaped if you use the method shown below. You will need a small, thin block of poly-styrene and a fine needle. Apply the fabric stiffener to the painted silk, and when dry, cut out the circles before the stiffener dries.

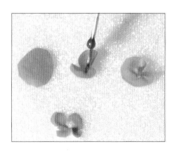

*Push each circle firmly into the thin block of polystyrene using a blunt point. Drip a small drop of fabric stiffener on to the silk circles and allow them to dry. Thread them on to a needle as shown above.*

Two circles, one slightly larger than the other, can be pinned on to the board together to make a fuller flower head. Roses, nasturtiums and many more flowers can be created in this way.

## Early Morning Poppies
### Eileen Burrell

*Eileen proves you do not have to fill every gap with stitches. The distant poppies*
*are worked in seeding stitch, the poppies in the middle distance are formed using*
*French knots, and the foreground poppies are made by threading small fabric*
*flower heads on to thread stems and restiffening them. The use of pale grey*
*chiffon gives a feeling of early morning mist.*

*145 x 125mm (5³/₄ x 4⁷/₈in)*

## Secret Door

### JENNY HEWINS

*Jenny planned and worked this embroidery in two pieces. First, she painted, stitched and stretched the
door on to mounting card. Then, she worked the frame and arch on a separate piece of fabric, and cut
out the door area. The door is then taped in position behind the arch. A fine piece of carefully bent wood
is attached to the inside of the arch, and then decorated with roses and hydrangeas. The roses are made
using the polystyrene method and the fern is stitched on to silk crepeline. Long and short straight stitch is
worked on the door. The wall is painted and decorated with straight stitch. The foreground is painted
and stitched to give the impression of paving stones.*

*200mm (8in) diameter*

*Detail of the embroidery opposite. The hydrangea flowers in the background are composed of many small pieces of silk fabric, threaded on to stems of green thread and then tied into bunches. The tall stems of pink lobelia in the foreground consist of lots of tiny flowers tied on to a pre-stiffened stem. Jenny has worked button hole bar on to the top of each stem to represent the unopened flowers.*

# Walled Garden

### JULIE ARMITAGE

*When an embroidery is as three-dimensional as this one, it is essential to work all the flat*
*background stitches first, otherwise the threads will get tangled up with the foreground foliage.*
*The wall is painted and embroidered with straight stitch. Lazy daisy stitch and French knots*
*are worked on top and the greenhouse is stitched in with long straight stitches. Tufted chives,*
*cold water soluble flowers, fabric lilies and fabric artichokes decorate the foreground. The tiny*
*pump was sliced in half by Julie's father and stitched in place before adding the foliage.*

*180mm (7in) diameter*

## ARUM LILY

Stiffened silk can be used to make more elaborate flowers. Lilies are a wonderful example of how silk can be made into more complicated forms. Here I show how to make the leaves and flowers separately. Twist the two stems to join them together.

Gently stiffen the fabric before starting to make the flowers. This makes it easier to cut, prevents it from fraying, and helps to maintain creases and folds. By bending the threads you can give the leaves a gentle curve, or make them turn at a right angle. Similar flowers and leaves are shown throughout the book.

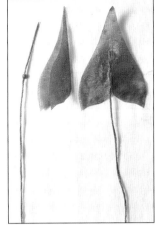

*Paint a small area of silk mottled green using a mixture of black and yellow poster paints (see pages 32 and 33). Dry the fabric and stiffen it. Cut out the leaf. Secure a piece of stiffened thread to the underside of the leaf with a few stitches.*

*Paint a piece of plain silk white, then stiffen it. (Painting the silk white will prevent it from becoming transparent when stiffened.) Cut a small circle, roll it on to the top of the stiffened thread, and secure it with fabric stiffener.*

*Detail of the lilies opposite*

# Cold water soluble fabric

Cold water soluble fabric is a clear material which can be used to great effect in landscapes, gardens and country scenes. The stitches are embroidered on to it in the normal way, and the fabric is then dissolved in cold water, leaving the embroidery free to be worked on to the picture. When stitching flowers, the more you work, the more secure the finished flower heads will be.

Place the fabric on top of the inner embroidery frame and place the outer ring on top. Tighten the screw. Be careful not to stretch the fabric as it will tear. To avoid this, a double layer could be used.

Bring your thread through to the front of the fabric, leaving a 12mm (¹/₂in) length loose on the back.

When the fabric has dissolved, carefully slide the daisy off the needle on to a non-absorbent surface to dry. Although the fabric will seem to have disappeared, it will have stiffened the thread. Any stray pieces of thread can be cut off when the daisy is completely dry. If some of the fabric is still visible, it is perfectly safe to repeat the process. The flower heads can now be threaded on to a stem and restiffened (see opposite).

If you have never stitched on cold water soluble fabric before, I suggest that you spend a little time working with it first. Now you have stitched your first daisy, you can experiment with different coloured threads and the stitches shown on pages 12 and 13. A variety of flowers and grasses can easily be worked on the fabric and they can be used to enhance your embroideries.

Here I show you how to stitch a flower head. If you want to stitch a grass head, start by making a lazy daisy stitch then cup it with two fly stitches. Keep the stitches close together so that they are almost stitched on top of each other. This ensures that the head will not fall apart when water is dripped on to it.

As you become more adept at using the fabric, you may find it quicker to put all of the stitched pieces into a sieve and to run cold water through them. A hair-dryer can be used to dry them, but take care they do not stick to the sieve.

Finally, keep the fabric in a dry place, and only buy a small quantity at a time, as after a while it tends to become brittle.

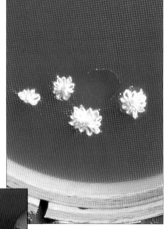

*Using lazy daisy stitch, embroider the petals, working opposite petals so that your thread passes back and forth across the middle of the daisy. This helps to hold the flower together. As you work, stitch over the loose thread at the back. Place a yellow French knot in the centre. Cut out the flower as close as possible to the thread.*

*Pick up the daisy head with a needle then carefully drip water on to it using a paint brush. As the fabric dissolves then dries, it stiffens the daisy and holds the flower together.*

## Daisies

### LYNN LEVER

*The distant hills are made from painted silk, slightly stiffened so that the fabric does not
fray. Lynn spent many weeks embroidering the daisies on to cold water soluble fabric.
She then threaded them on to stems and attached them to the foreground. It is the sheer
mass of daisies that makes this simple embroidery so lovely.*

*180mm (7in) diameter*

# *Leaves*

Stiffened fabric can be used in the landscape to create many different kinds of foliage.

### *Step 1*

Pour a small amount of yellow poster paint into a palette. Add a little black paint and mix gently with plenty of water to make a murky green, which should be either a shade darker or a shade lighter than the green threads you have been using.

### *Step 2*

Carefully brush the paint on to the silk, making sure you give the impression of stained, not painted, silk.

### *Step 3*

Add a few strokes of yellow and vary the shades of green slightly. Do not worry if the paint has a blotchy appearance. Grasses and leaves are made up of different shades of green.

### *Step 4*

Once the silk is dry, brush on a thin solution of fabric stiffener. The silk will be easier to cut once it has been stiffened, and will not fray. Hang the silk up to dry. Do not leave it on a flat surface while it is wet.

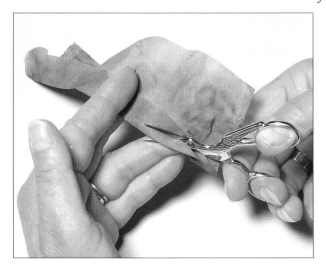

### Step 5

Using a pair of small, sharp scissors, cut out the leaves. The painted silk can be folded, to create leaves like those shown here. These can be stitched on to the foregrounds of your embroideries.

Alternatively you can cut long fine blades of grass. Try to use a single cut for each blade, as a staggered cut will produce a rather crooked blade. Cut a number of blades, in lengths varying from 12–37mm ($^1/_2$–1$^1/_2$in). As grass grows in clumps, stitch them on to your embroidery in groups. Position the long grasses to fill any gap and come between, rather than cover, any flowers. Place groups of shorter grasses under the flowers, making sure that all the blades are 'growing' from the base of your work. Attach each blade with a single stitch. The greater the variety of leaves you cut, the more interesting your embroidery will be.

*A piece of painted, stiffened and folded silk is cut out, and trimmed into a realistic leaf shape. This is then attached to a piece of florist's wire or a stiffened thread. Groups of these leaves can be attached to the foreground fabric of your embroideries with tiny stitches.*

*Painted and stiffened silk is cut out to create a selection of leaves and grasses.*

# Walled Garden

## DOROTHY PERRYMAN

*This embroidery and Julie Armitage's Walled Garden on page 28, were inspired by the same subject. However, they have both been interpreted in different ways. A few weeks before commencing the embroidery, Dorothy attended a course on how to make miniature figures. She wanted to put her new-found knowledge to use and so she added the gardener. The wheelbarrow, door hinges and catch were made by her husband, Charles.*

*280mm (11in) diameter*

## Sweetpeas

### FIONA BATEMAN

*A greenhouse gives this embroidery a simple but effective background. All Fiona's efforts have
gone into making the multitude of leaves, nasturtiums and sweetpeas. The small marrows in
the corner of the garden are made out of modelling clay which has been hardened in the oven
(see page 70), and Fiona has made the sweetpea canes from florist's wire.*

*125 x 125mm (4⁷/₈ x 4⁷/₈in)*

# Grasses

It is easy to create the impression of a million grass heads in a field. Grass heads can be stitched straight on to your picture using a variety of shades of green. Mix them so that darker grasses show up against a pale green background and pale green grasses show up against a dark green background. Grasses can also be made separately and stitched on to the foreground of your embroidery. On page 30, I explain how to make grass heads using the cold water soluble method. Here I show how to create grasses using knots and a hand crochet method. Both are equally effective and can be used in a variety of ways to add interest and depth to your embroideries.

## KNOTTED THREAD

Simple stiffened threads, or threads with knots tied in the ends, give the impression of grasses. These can be added to embroideries and look effective nestling amongst flowers and foliage.

*Tie a knot into the end of a trimmed strand of dark green thread. Stiffen the thread with fabric stiffener. Tie a number of these threads together and attach them to the embroidery with small running stitches.*

## HAND CROCHET

This is a simple way of crocheting a chain with your fingers, which avoids the use of a crochet hook. The embroidery opposite shows a good example of the hand crocheted chain. The grasses in the foreground are all made using this method.

*Wind the thread around your fingers.*

*Pull the thread through.*

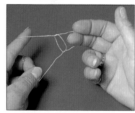

*Complete the knot, and then repeat the process until a chain is formed. This will be the grass head. Trim the stem.*

*This barley is made using a hand crocheted chain. Lengths of thread are pulled through the chain with a needle. These are then stiffened, secured in a point and trimmed.*

## Cornflowers
### FIONA BATEMAN

*The foreground grasses are worked using the hand crochet method shown on this page. The embroidery is a good example of what you can do if you cannot crochet with a hook! The trees in the distance and middle distance are stitched using French knots and fly stitch. The field is worked in straight stitch, and the flowers are made using cold water soluble fabric and painted silk. The cornflowers are tufts of blue thread, attached to green threads and stiffened.*

*140 x 185mm (5$^1$/$_2$ x 7$^1$/$_4$in)*

# Trees

Trees are an important part of the landscape, and they come in all shapes, sizes and colours. The time of day and the position of the sun will alter their colour and hue. Look at a tree with the sun behind it, then look at the same tree with the sun shining on it. The light gives it more colour and shadow. All this is important when you come to decide how to embroider your trees.

Texture is equally important. Do you work a tree using French knots, fly stitch or lazy daisy stitch? Twelve trees all stitched using French knots in the same shade or colour, would not be interesting, whereas if you were to add more shades and colours or alter your stitch, you would immediately have a more appealing embroidery.

If you study a tree from different viewpoints, it will become apparent that this same tree can be embroidered in different ways. Stand beside it and the leaves will appear quite large, so you could use tiny fabric leaves on your picture to represent them. Walk away and look back, and the leaves will appear smaller, therefore lazy daisy stitch would be more appropriate. Walk further away still, and the leaves will become even more indistinct. French knots would be ideal for portraying this distant foliage.

## Stitched trees

In the Cornfield embroidery (see page 19), the distant tree was worked in fly stitch and French knots. This is a simple way of showing trees in the distance. Use one strand of thread and use one large fly stitch for the trunk and main branches. Smaller stitches can be used for the rest of the branches. The fly stitches should be staggered, rather than joined to the main trunk at the same spot. In the picture below, the trees and bushes are embroidered on to a painted winter sky using fly stitch.

The picture opposite shows how stitches can also be used to create trees in the middle distance. Lazy daisy stitch is used to give the impression of foliage on the two damson trees. Hessian is used for the trunks and branches, and the leaves are stitched around the tops of the trees.

### Sheep in Winter
MARY LITTLE

*Mary has created a snow scene using just a few stitches. When you work a simple embroidery like this, the stitches have to be right first time. A poorly worked tree cannot be covered up and errors are clearly visible.*

*135 x 150mm (5³/₈ x 5⁷/₈in)*

## *View Through the Kitchen Garden*

### HELEN BARNETT

*This is Helen's view of her own kitchen garden. It is full of interest and she has tried to include everything, including her potted chives in front of the greenhouse, the straw-protected strawberries beside the path, and the giant rhubarb leaves. French knots are used on the distant trees. It is essential to work more detail into the damson trees which overshadow the garden gate, because they are nearer. Hessian is used for the trunks and branches instead of fly stitch, and the leaves are embroidered on to the fabric using lazy daisy stitch instead of French knots.*

*170 x 150mm (6⁵/₈ x 5⁷/₈in)*

# Trees with blossom

This is a good example of how flowers can enhance a simple scene. The elderflower tree is embroidered on to a background of painted silk, with only the leaves and flowers visible. The tree trunk and branches are hidden beneath a blanket of foliage. Tiny elderflowers are stitched on top of lazy daisy stitched leaves using clusters of French knots. The detail on this page shows how each flower head is worked and placed amongst the leaves. The white of these flowers is echoed in the foreground flowers which are worked on cold water soluble fabric and attached to stiffened stems. The mount is an important part of the finished picture, with its arched surround.

There are more examples of trees with blossom in this section. Two fruit blossom trees are the main feature of the embroidery on page 50. The three-dimensional flowers are made from small pieces of plain white silk, painted white, then stiffened. Many flowers are cut out, attached to small green stems, then stitched on to the hessian branches, some of which have been stiffened and curved to give a three-dimensional effect.

On page 51, cherry blossom spreads across the embroidery. French knots are embroidered on to the fabric background initially, then they are built up with cold water soluble French knots.

There are many ways of portraying blossom. Use the stitches on pages 12 and 13 and the techniques illustrated in this section and experiment with different threads.

*A detail of the embroidery opposite, showing the leaves and blossom.*

## Elderflower

MARION BARWELL

*Marion did not want any branches to show on her tree, so she embroidered many elderflower heads using French knots. The grass is worked in straight stitch and small pieces of wood make up the gate in the foreground.*

*165 x 205mm (6¹/₂ x 8¹/₈in)*

41

# *Thread trees*

Twisted threads can produce interesting textures. Here the threads are used to create a winter tree against a painted silk and chiffon background. Shades of brown are entwined thickly at the base of the trunk; they gradually fan out into branches.

Edna Tait has used these threads because she likes using pure silks. She has taken twelve stranded threads and couched them down along the tree trunk to help create texture. As the threads travel up the trunk they fan out gradually. If you follow a thread from the base of the trunk up and along a branch, you will see that she continued to split the thread until it was impossible to split it any further.

## *Icelandic Tree*
### EDNA TAIT

*Loaned by kind permission of John and Ursula Hibbert. This tree was seen in the middle of a frozen wilderness in Iceland. To give the glow of a pink sunset, Edna has sewn pink chiffon on to the tree and snow using pink seeding stitches. For the foreground she has used invisible thread to sew pink chiffon on to the ruched up white silk.*

*240mm (9¹/₂in) diameter*

# Cold water soluble trees

You have learnt how to embroider a small tree, and a larger thread tree. Now try stitching on to cold water soluble fabric. The right hand tree, behind the wisteria, was embroidered using this technique. It gives a chunky look to a tree full of foliage. If you were to work five or six pieces like this, you would then have many layers and boughs on a tree.

## House on Lake Como

### MARION LEWIS

*The trees on the left are worked straight on to the painted silk background using French knots and lazy daisy stitch. The tree on the right is worked on cold water soluble fabric. The wisteria is also worked on cold water soluble fabric and attached to twisted hessian branches. The toothpick fence is decorated with florist's wire and the bricks are made from small rectangles of card covered in silk. Marion worked this picture from a photograph taken by her husband.*

*210 x 185mm (8 1/4 x 7 1/4in)*

# Hessian trees

One of the most valuable new discoveries for my students and I has been hessian trees. Like most ideas it was found by accident.

I have a dog named Scruffy. One day, I was chatting to a friend in my kitchen when Scruffy, as usual, decided to join in the conversation! It became impossible to talk, so Scruffy was banned to the dining room, where I had a hessian runner in front of the patio doors leading to the garden. Instead of going outside, Scruffy decided it would be far more interesting to play with the runner. By the time I realised what was happening, it was in shreds. In disgust, I threw the hessian down beside the front door, planning to remove it to the garage. As I showed my friend out, I looked up at my Clematis Montana which was trying to fight its way through the front door – and I looked down at the runner. The idea for the hessian trees and creepers was born.

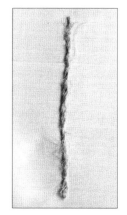

*Eileen Burrell worked this sample which shows how to split the threads.*

*Here is Scruffy. Without him I would not have thought of using hessian.*

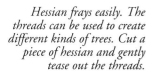

*Hessian frays easily. The threads can be used to create different kinds of trees. Cut a piece of hessian and gently tease out the threads.*

*If you wish to make more three-dimensional trees or branches, you need to stiffen the hessian with fabric stiffener. Gently brush the solution on to each thread with a needle.*

*Make sure all the branches are covered with the solution, and leave to dry. Now you can couch the tree on to your embroidery.*

## Winter Crab Apples

### Julie Armitage

*A hessian tree is stitched on to a painted background and one layer of fine pink silk is laid over it. The foreground tree is then worked on top of this. Twisted, stiffened hessian branches are decorated with giant French knots, which are also worked into the grass at the base of the embroidery.*

*110 x 140mm (4³/₈ x 5¹/₂in)*

## Tree and Sunset
### BETTY STOCKWELL

*Loaned by kind permission of Sheila Wallwork, Knutsford. Betty's tree shows how effective a simple tree can look on a colour-washed background. Because the hessian was slightly stiffened it was not necessary to stitch the fine branches down. All Betty had to do was stitch the trunk.*

*120 x 120mm (4³/₄ x 4³/₄in)*

## Small Trees
### EILEEN BURRELL

*The hessian used on the two trees shown here is not stiffened. The threads are attached to the fabric using tiny stitches.*

*Small silver stitches are worked into ruched-up silk to give an impression of snow.*
*60 x 60mm (2³/₈ x 2³/₈in)*

*Silver stitches are embroidered on the tree to give an impression of frost.*
*60 x 60mm (2³/₈ x 2³/₈in)*

## Winter Hedge

PAMELA SARGEANT

*Hedges in winter look wonderful. You can see the way they grow, the way they are cut and laid,
and the gaps where animals have pushed their way through. Pam carefully studied a hedge before
creating this simple scene. Folds of white satin create the snow.*

*215mm (8¹/₂in) diameter*

## Bluebell Wood

### JEAN MILLS

*Loaned by kind permission of Heather Stevenson, Broxbourne. The view at the end of the arch of trees and the carpet of bluebells were stitched first. Jean then couched in the hessian trees, starting at the back of the wood and working forward. The three-dimensional foliage in the foreground is made using tiny pieces of blue and green stained silk.*

*155 x 205mm (6¹/₈ x 8in).*

## Bluebell Wood

### VIVIEN TAYLOR

*Masses of fluffy tufting brings Vivien's embroidery to life. Another texture is brought into the picture with the addition of the beautifully cut leaves in the foreground.*

*240mm (9¹/₂in) diameter*

*Cherry Blossom*

Ann Barker

*The blossom is worked on a background of green chiffon which overlays the painted sky. Cold water soluble French knots are added to the small flowers to build up the texture. Twisted hessian forms the tree trunk and the fence consists of toothpicks and dark green thread. The mount and frame are part of your embroidery, so always feel you can bring the embroidery on to the mount.*

*125 x 105mm (4⁷/₈ x 4¹/₈in)*

## Buttercups and Blossom

Carol Allan

Opposite

*The fabric flowers are all made using the method described on page 24. The buttercup buds are made by tying small yellow knots on to green threads.*

*180 x 220mm (7 x 8⁵/₈in)*

# Silk shapes

Silk can be used in different ways to enhance your embroideries. Brick walls, a vase, a chimney pot and even an old car are shown in this section as examples of what you can do with silk. It is a simple technique which can add depth, perspective and interest to a scene. Here, I show how to build up a wall from small pieces of silk stretched over card.

Once you have built your first wall, experiment with other colours. If you want a red brick wall, paint some silk with red poster paint, mixed with a little yellow. Splatter a variety of shades over the silk until they all seem to blend into each other. Try flicking your paint brush on to the silk to give a lovely speckled effect. Another way to apply the paint is to dilute it and transfer it to a non-absorbent surface such as glass. Drop the dry silk on to the paint, pick it up, then drop it again. Continue doing this until your silk is completely coloured. Because the paint is resting on a non-absorbent surface, it forms globules and interesting effects can be achieved.

Flowers, grasses and moss can be embroidered over and in between the padded silk bricks or stones to hide any untidy joins or gaps. There are several examples in this section, including the embroidery opposite, which shows flowers tumbling over the bricks into the pond, and the Grecian Urn embroidery on page 54, which includes small tufts of grass in between the padded paving stones. If you choose to decorate your silk stones in this way, do not worry about disturbing any threads when you cut them out, particularly if the stitches you are using are seeded or French knots. It is unlikely that any of your work will come undone.

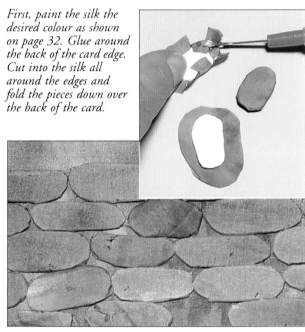

*First, paint the silk the desired colour as shown on page 32. Glue around the back of the card edge. Cut into the silk all around the edges and fold the pieces down over the back of the card.*

*Make enough bricks to build a small wall. Attach each brick to the silk background using tiny seeding stitches in the corners. This wall is stitched on to the fabric behind the daisies in the embroidery on page 31.*

## Conservatory

### JEAN GREEN

*Loaned with kind permission of Nigel and Pat Barry, Selbourne. The garden in the background consists of straight stitch, French knots and fly stitch. The stone wall and urn are shaped pieces of card covered with stained silk. The small curly threads in the foreground are made by twisting pieces of thread around a knitting needle. They are then stiffened, removed from the needle when dry, and attached to the embroidery. Fine pieces of wood, which were taken from an old table mat, make up the conservatory itself and most of the vine stems are hessian. The finer leaf stems are single strands of thread and the grapes are worked on cold water soluble fabric.*

*190 x 130mm (7¹/₂ x 5in)*

## Stone Sink
### MAUREEN CLUNIE

*The brick wall is painted with a flat-ended watercolour paint brush. The Virginia Creeper's hessian stems are stitched on to the wall and the silk for the leaves is splattered with a variety of shades so that each leaf is a different shape. The shaped sink is filled with cold water soluble fabric flowers, and foliage.*

*150 x 115mm (5$^7$/$_8$ x 4$^1$/$_2$in)*

## Grecian Urn
### MARGARET MCNEENEY
*Opposite*

*Margaret painted the silk, seeded it all over to give texture, stitched on small pieces of multi-coloured chiffon, then stretched pieces of the embroidered fabric over small rectangles of card to form the bricks. The vase is also made using this method, and the paving stones are painted, but not embroidered. The daisies consist of tiny fabric flower heads attached to green threads. The ivy leaves are attached to a green thread, then stitched into place.*

*180 x 130mm (7 x 5$^1$/$_8$in)*

## Chimney Pot

### HELEN ROBINSON

*Helen embroidered the wall with white long and short stitch, then constructed the trellis
using fine wood from an old table mat. The chimney is a piece of thin cardboard which
is cut to shape, bent, and then covered with painted silk. Tufted flowers decorate the
foreground; the foxgloves are worked on cold water soluble fabric; and tiny white
flowers, made using the polystyrene method, peep out of the chimney pot.*

*180mm (7in) diameter*

## *Tree Stump*

### JANE HETHERINGTON

*The tree stump is composed of layers of cardboard which are covered with painted silk and embroidered. The silk is stretched over the shaped pieces of cardboard and stitched into place. Lots of pieces of cold water soluble lichen are tucked in between and over the layers of silk. The toadstools are made from stiffened suede.*

*170 x 120mm (6⅝ x 4¾in)*

## Graveyard

### JULIE ARMITAGE

*This embroidery was constructed in many separate pieces and then assembled. All the tomb stones are made from pieces of card covered in painted silk. The flowers and foliage are tucked, draped and dripped over the stones, giving the illusion of neglect. The light at the back of the embroidery gives a highly dramatic effect.*

*250mm (9⁷/₈in) diameter*

## Back to Nature

### JUDITH MASON

*This lovely old car is made from cardboard covered with painted silk. French knot trees are worked against a painted background and the cold water soluble bracken decorates the foreground. The stiffened hessian tree growing up through the car, has bunches of cold water soluble lazy daisy stitches tied to it.*

*155 x 115mm (6$^{1}$/$_{8}$ x 4$^{1}$/$_{2}$in)*

# Using other fabrics

Fine fabrics can be used to add atmosphere to embroideries. They can also be used as a base on which you can attach borders of three-dimensional flowers and foliage as on page 69, or floral bowers, as in the embroidery on pages 64–67.

## Chiffon

Chiffon can be used in many ways. You can use it to create misty scenes, or shafts of sunlight as on the opposite page. Here, two lengths of chiffon are laid down between the background and foreground to give an impression of the sun streaming through leafy branches. The chiffon is trapped between the mount and the hessian branches. The colour of the fabric reflects the green shady tones amongst the trees.

You can also embroider on chiffon to produce layers of stitches. If you do this, you must apply fabric stiffener to the back before you cut any unwanted chiffon away. The embroidery below shows layers of chiffon overlaid with embroidery. You can also use chiffon instead of cold water soluble fabric or silk crepeline.

*Tree in Tuscany*
JILL MILNE

*Loaned with kind permission of Brian and Winifred Edwards. This embroidery was inspired by a painting by Jill's son, Dan after a visit to Tuscany. Layers of coloured chiffon, overlaid with straight stitch and a few French knot trees, are used to give texture and a subtle change of colours. The foreground tree is stitched on to another band of stained silk, which has chiffon and French knots sewn on to it.*

*120 x 115mm (4³/₄ x 4¹/₂in)*

## Bluebell Wood

JEAN FELL

*The shafts of sunlight consists of two lengths of yellow chiffon. Masses of stiffened threads and buttonhole bar bluebells are used to fill in the foreground area.*

*215 x 155mm (8$^1$/$_2$ x 6$^1$/$_8$in)*

# Silk crepeline

Silk crepeline is an extremely fine, but strong fabric and it is very versatile. I was told about it by two fabric conservationists who supply the stiffener that my students and I use. They approached me and asked if crepeline would be of any use to us. As we were having difficulties finding sufficient supplies of the right shade of chiffon, I said yes.

Silk crepeline can be stained with different colours, to complement all the different thread shades used in your embroideries. Also, if you are stitching large areas, it is much easier to work with than cold water soluble fabric, which I tend to use for smaller items such as individual flower heads and grasses. Stitches can be worked on it, turned over and stiffened with fabric stiffener. They can then be cut out and sewn on to your embroidery. Stiffening the back ensures that if you accidentally cut a thread, the stitches will not come undone.

In the following pages I show how an embroidery can be enhanced with this fabric. The tree shown on this page was stitched on to silk crepeline, then it was stiffened on the back, so that when it was cut out it was able to stand up by itself. It screens part of the cottage which was worked in three parts to give a more three-dimensional feel.

The Laburnum Walk on page 64 shows how to build up layers of laburnum flowers which are stitched on to silk crepeline. French knots are worked on to the fabric in multi-shaded threads. The embroidered areas are cut out and attached to the background fabric with tiny running stitches. This is an effective way of building up texture and perspective.

*Detail of the embroidery opposite, showing fabric leaves and hessian branches stitched on to silk crepeline.*

## Woodland Cottage

### CAROL FARQUHAR

*The background trees are embroidered using fly stitch and French knots; and the cottage and windows are worked separately, and then taped together. Florists' wire forms the window panes and the foreground consists of a layer of three-dimensional flowers and foliage.*

*235 x 235mm (9¹/₄ x 9¹/₄in)*

## FLOWERS ON SILK CREPELINE

This embroidery was inspired by a magazine picture of the laburnum walk at Bodnant, in Wales. Liz Collishaw found the rich yellows of the hanging flowers so beautiful, that she could not resist the urge to embroider them.

The silk on the upper section of the walkway is painted using a mixture of yellows and greens. Similarly coloured threads are worked on to the silk, with straight stitch and French knots stitched over the arches. The pathway is worked in multi-coloured straight stitch, with a painted fabric wall along the left, carefully stitched to create a stone effect. Small French knots are used on the flower heads in the borders which contain a mixture of lazy daisy stitches, and three-dimensional flowers and foliage. Hessian stems wind themselves around the arches of wood and wire and are worked into the flowers above.

It was necessary to use three mounts for this embroidery. Liz needed to secure her layers of laburnum to a base that would enable her to lift them up, otherwise they would have lain flat on top of her background embroidery, which would have been far less dramatic.

*The three mounts complement the colours used in the embroidery. The laburnum flowers are stitched on to stretched silk crepeline in layers. French knots are worked on to the fabric in long clusters, then cut out at the bottom and removed from the frame. Painted fabric leaves are sewn along the top of each layer, amongst the hanging flowers.*

*This is the embroidery before the layers are attached. You could mount and frame it at this stage. The layers are optional, but they do add a wonderful three-dimensional feel.*

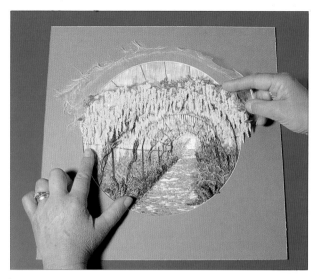

## FINISHING OFF

Two mounts, 355mm (14in) square, are used. The diameter of the inner circle is 235mm (9¼in). The outer circle is slightly larger, so that the double mount is visible.

### Step 1

Double-sided tape is positioned around the top of the inner mount. The silk crepeline, with its stitched flowers and fabric leaves, is placed over the tape and pressed down firmly.

### Step 2

The second layer of silk crepeline and stitching is stretched on to the back of the top mount using double-sided tape. Small polystyrene blocks are glued down on either side and in the centre, to hold the embroidery away from the background. The blocks can be as deep as you like. The silk crepeline could be as much as 25mm (1in) away from the background, to give an even more three-dimensional feel.

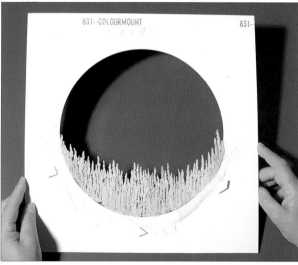

### Step 3

The mount is turned over and carefully positioned on top of the embroidery, so that all the edges match and the laburnum falls naturally over the background. The two mounts are then taped securely together.

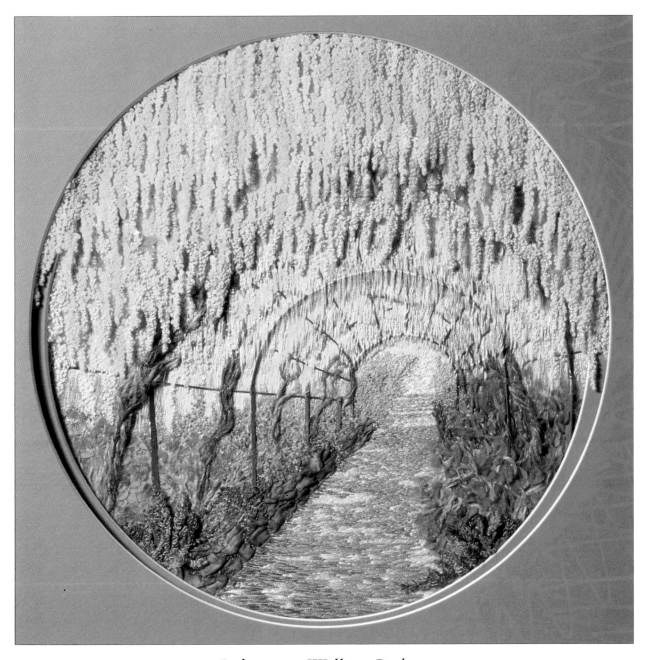

### Laburnum Walk at Bodnant

*Liz Collishaw*

*The finished embroidery incorporating the two mounts.*

*245mm (9⁵/₈in) diameter*

## SILK CREPELINE FOLIAGE

Silk crepeline is used as a base for the grass border along the front of the cottage (see above). The fabric is stretched on to a hoop and all the flowers and foliage are stitched in a band across it. The hoop is turned over, the back of the stitches are stiffened, and the band is then cut out.

The cottage is worked on painted silk which is embroidered, cut out and folded around card. Three-dimensional flowers and foliage are added afterwards.

### Step 2

Foxgloves are sewn on to the painted door.

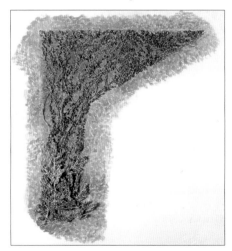

### Step 1

The embroidery is worked on a painted, mottled green background. Hessian threads form the stems which decorate the background, along with lazy daisy stitch and French knot foliage. The variegated tree is stitched on to cold water soluble fabric.

### Step 3

A square-ended brush is used to paint the bricks. They are then haphazardly stitched over with multi-shaded threads, using straight stitch. Hessian threads are stitched on, then painted silk leaves are sewn on to the branches. More foxgloves and cold water soluble fabric foliage are added.

## Woodcutter's Cottage
### JEAN FELL

*The whole embroidery gives a feeling of rich, dense flowers and foliage growing randomly over a secluded cottage. The colours used on the cottage complement the colours in the flowers. Greys and shades of green and pink adorn the walls, together with a smattering of darker hues.*

*270 x 220mm (10⅝ x 8⅝in)*

# Miniature objects

Embroideries can be made more interesting with the addition of miniature items. Tiny garden tools, miniatures from doll's house suppliers, small pebbles, toothpicks and florist's wire can all be used to add interest to your scene. If you want to make your own objects, fruit and vegetables can be made from oven-drying modelling clay which is available from most craft shops. To attach the hardened clay, pass a needle and thread through the item you have made just before it is fired. If the object is too small, gently press the thread on to the back, then put it in the oven. In the embroidery on page 35, this type of clay has been used to make the cucumbers in the vegetable patch. If you want to complement the colours in your embroidery, white clay can be bought, which you can then colour yourself.

Wire, wood and string can also be used effectively. Greenhouses and pergolas can be made using wire covered with fabric; matchsticks, lollipop sticks and wood from modelling shops can be turned into fences and trellises; and twigs from the garden can be used to made garden furniture.

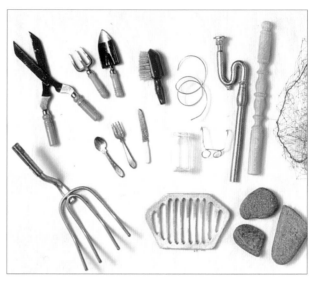

*With a little imagination, miniature objects can be used effectively to complement landscapes and garden scenes. The tiny pebbles here were found on a beach and the other items were all bought from a doll's house supplier. All these items can be attached to the background fabric using complementary coloured thread and a few discrete stitches.*

## The Bell

ROWINA TOPHAM

*Rowina made the pewter bell and created the garland of leaves by stitching hundreds of tiny fabric leaves on to silk crepeline. The bell is suspended from a small piece of wood with string and the garland is glued on to the mount.*

*160mm (6¹/4in) diameter*

## Lazy Summer Days
### Leila Sutcliffe

*The tiny chair provides the focal point of this embroidery. It is made from fine wood,
which was purchased from a model shop, and it has been washed with white paint. The
hat is made from builder's scrim and moulded over a thimble.*

*115 x 150mm (4¹/₂ x 5⁷/₈in)*

71

## Houses in Tuscany
### JILL MILNE

*Jill made the houses out of porcelain, then coloured and fired them. She made small holes in each of the houses so that she could stitch them securely to the painted silk background. The cypress trees are worked on cold water soluble fabric and stitched on to the field.*

*185mm(7¹/₄in)*

## Kitchen Garden

### JO JOHNSTON

*French knots are worked against a background of painted silk. The canes are formed out of
florist's wire, with stiffened thread twisted around them. Toothpicks lean against the
greenhouse, which is made out of one strand of white thread. The vegetables are made out of
stiffened fabric and the cauliflowers are French knots worked on cold water soluble fabric.
Crumpled grey silk and small pebbles form the soil, and a small fork is stitched on to the
embroidery, with part of it coming out over the mount.*

*145mm (5³/₄in) diameter*

## Italian Garden

### JUNE WALTON

*All the trellis work is made from very fine wood which was bought from a model shop. Sometimes, as in this instance, it is easier to use wood as an alternative to thread. It gives a closer cut line as well as a solid base, which is excellent if you want to twist stems or trunks around a firm shape. Adding lots of different textures often makes the finished piece look more interesting, and this is an important element in an embroidery such as this. Always remember that you can add or remove things at any stage. Here, the little bay trees in the pots were not in the original embroidery, but were added at a later date. June felt the foreground needed enhancing, and that a classical garden would look better with ornaments or pots.*

*245 x 170mm (9⅝ x 6⅝in)*

## USING SMALL STONES

Stones can be interpreted in a number of different ways. They can be painted directly on to the silk and decorated with small stitches, or they can be made from shaped card and painted silk, like the bricks on page 52. They can also be embroidered.

If you use real stones, they can add authenticity to your finished picture. It was thanks to a student named May that I accidentally discovered an excellent way of attaching the stones to the embroideries.

May visited me to ask how she could sew some boulders into a raging river. We were thinking about the answer to this problem while emptying some drawers. Suddenly, some very fine chiffon material fell on the floor beside a Dolly Varden style bag. I had found the answer! It was to make a bag from chiffon, inside which the stone could be held securely. This could then be attached to the embroidery easily using a few tiny stitches.

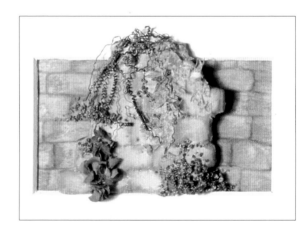

*Ann painted the brick wall using a flat paint brush. She then painted another piece of brick wall, which she stretched over a piece of padded cardboard. Green and cream paint has been flicked on to while silk with a brush to give an impression of variegated ivy. The tendrils in the centre of the boulder are made by stiffening a thread, twisting around a needle while it is still wet, and removing it when it is dry.*

*90 x 50mm (3¹/₂ x 2in)*

## *Rockery*

### ANN BARKER

*The four embroideries on this page have been worked by Ann. Each one is a separate picture, but they are all mounted on one board. At the top of the page, real stones are held in place by little chiffon bags. Ann was able to work French knots on to the chiffon with the help of cold water soluble fabric.*

*200 x 40mm (7⁷/₈ x 1¹/₂in)*

Ann stained the silk and ironed it on to a stiffening fabric. She was then able to cut out the bricks without fear of them fraying. The two layers of material give the bricks a certain depth. Cold water soluble saxifrage is embroidered on top of the bricks, and white alyssum tumbles down the left hand side in a cascade of white French knots.

*180 x 100mm (7 x 3⁷/₈in)*

The large boulder is padded and embroidered with French knots. The tiny stones, which Ann found on holiday, are held in place using needleweaving and invisible thread.

*115 x 80mm (4¹/₂ x 3¹/₈in)*

## Seashore

EVELYN ROSS

*A chiffon shore, decorated with seeding stitch and French knots, rests against a painted sky. The stones are held in chiffon bags and attached to the fabric. The silk cliffs and brown distant rocks are slightly stiffened to stop them fraying.*

*75mm (6⁷/₈in) diameter*

# Mounts

Finishing off an embroidery is important, and the mounting and framing can make all the difference to a stitched scene. A double mount prevents the embroidery from being squashed against the glass. If the embroidery is three-dimensional you have to use an even larger number of mounts. Alternatively, you could insert a small block, either between the glass and the mount, or between the mount and the embroidery, in order to lift the glass up.

Mounts should be carefully selected to complement the colours of the embroidery. In particular, avoid any bright colours that could clash.

## Dank Wood

ANN BARKER

*This is such a dark, atmospheric embroidery, that Ann and I found it difficult to find a mount to offset the scene. Most mounts seemed to look too clean. Finally, Ann decided to offset the inner mount, so she stippled paint on to the outer one, thereby subtly introducing colour from the embroidery itself.*

*Ann uses layers of chiffon on top of hessian trees and stitches to push the background further into the distance, and to give the impression of a dark wood. The small group of daffodils is highlighted by using a bright yellow thread and by stitching in chiffon to create shafts of sunlight. A variety of threads are used to build up the textured tree trunk. The old bracken in the foreground is worked on cold water soluble fabric.*

*140 x 175mm (5 1/2 x 6 5/sin)*

79

# Drawing on a mount

This embroidery has been worked by Leila Sutcliffe. It has been beautifully mounted, with the colours complementing the embroidery and the pathway extending down over the foreground area. Leila wanted to bring the embroidery out on to the mount, so she painted flag stones on the mounting card to add perspective. The rich reds and warm pinks are reflected in the surround, and the arch mount is an ideal choice for the subject.

The flowers in the embroidery are attached to stiffened green thread stems. It is Leila we have to thank for introducing us to this technique. My students and I had always included flowers in our work, but we had not thought to attach them to lengths of thread. That small step added so much to our embroideries. This method is used in many areas in the opposite scene. The blossom overhanging the wooden arch, the leaves on the little maple tree and the magnolia flowers are all small pieces of fabric attached to stiffened stems by small threads.

The two small walls on either side were painted and embroidered, before being stitched on to the background fabric. The flag stones were painted, embroidered, then cut out and stretched over pieces of cardboard that were trimmed to the correct shape. The three plant pots were then added.

*Detail of the embroidery opposite. The texture on the flag stones is made by stippling a paint brush on to the mount. The little blossom petals are stitched, rather than glued, on to the mounting card.*

*Detail of the embroidery opposite. The little magnolia flowers are attached in exactly the same way that poppies are attached to stems. They have been allowed to droop over the mount. There are so many varieties of coloured mounts on the market to choose from. See what is available, try different combinations, paint on the mounts, and experiment with colours.*

## Japanese Garden

LEILA SUTCLIFFE

*The rich reds and warm pinks of the embroidery are reflected in the colour of the mount.*

*300 x 320mm (11³/₄ x 12⁵/₈in)*

# Layering mounts

If you want to create an impression of depth in your embroideries, you can layer your mounts as shown here. The clematis flowers falling over the outer mount and the flowers in the foreground add to the three-dimensional feel.

This design, created by Leila Sutcliffe, was worked out on paper first. There are four sections to the embroidery and they are each worked on a circular frame. The silk is removed when the embroidery is finished and cut to shape, before being glued around card. The whole embroidery is then decorated with tiny flowers and long grasses.

## Step 2

Paint the silk in shades of green, to form a background for the flowers. Stitch clematis flowers on to the arch base. Stitch silk crepeline grasses beneath the embroidery. Use lengths of string for the clematis stems. Place the long threads of clematis in position over the arch and attach them to the background fabric with tiny stitches using dark green thread.

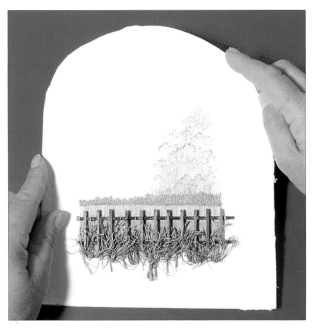

## Step 1

Paint the sky with light blue poster paint and paint the green tree on top when the silk is dry. Use fly stitches and French knots to portray branches and leaves, and for the field, use straight stitches topped with French knots. To make the fence, attach stained toothpicks and small bits of wood to the fabric with tiny stitches in a matching thread. Stitch stiffened green threads along the bottom of the fence.

*The clematis are made the same way as the poppies on page 24. They are stitched on to stiffened, twisted threads. Small leaves are cut out of green stiffened fabric and sewn amongst the many flower heads.*

### Step 4

Remove the work; draw a line around the arch, using the marks as a guide.

### Step 3

Remove the embroidery from the frame and stretch it on to card. Place it over a large piece of white card and prick the shape of the arch through.

*Detail of the above embroidery. Be careful when pricking the arch. Take care to avoid the flower heads and the thread stems.*

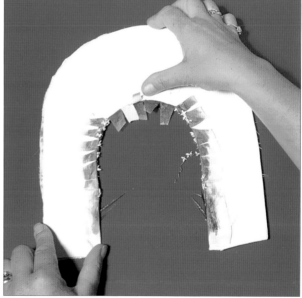

### Step 5

Cut out the arch and place the embroidery upside down on the work surface. Place the arch on the back of the embroidery and cut around it, leaving 20mm (³/₄in) within the shape. Cut into the 20mm (³/₄in) silk edge and glue this down around the arch using paper adhesive. When the glue is dry, turn the embroidery around and place in on the background.

## Step 6

To complete the embroidery, place tiny bunches of flowers in between the mounts. These will cover any gaps that have not been filled with stitches. At this stage you can 'play' with the embroidery. You could decide to place the flowers on either the left or right; you could tuck a few smaller flowers in front of the fence, or trail a stem of clematis over it; you could make a gate from florist's wire to span the path in front of the scene.

There are so many things that can be added, but there comes a stage when you have to make a decision about what to include and what to leave out. Another of my students has worked this same embroidery, but stitched cold water soluble wisteria over the arch.

*Clematis*

LEILA SUTCLIFFE

*The finished embroidery, with all the flowers in position.*

*280 x 250mm (11 x 9⁷/₈in)*

## Wisteria Walk

### MAUREEN CLUNIE

*This embroidery is also worked in four stages. The more confidence you gain, the
more steps you will want to probably incorporate in your scenes. If you study the way
the Clematis was assembled (see pages 82–85) you will see that this embroidery has
been constructed in the same way. Maureen chose this subject because of the dramatic
colour of the cornfield in the background. To make it more atmospheric she added in
a few layers of mauve chiffon.*

*250 x 220mm (9⁷/₈ x 8⁵/₈in)*

## Italian Courtyard

### LEILA SUTCLIFFE

*This is another four-part embroidery. The little alcove was embroidered on one
hoop, the ornate arch was worked on a second hoop, and the main wall, with its
hollyhocks and wisteria, was worked on a third hoop. The embroidered flagstones are
stained using fabric dyes. After they were embroidered they were cut into small pieces
and stretched over shaped cardboard. The curls of hessian are created by twisting
hessian threads around large needles, coating them with fabric stiffener, and allowing
them to dry before removing them.*

*240 x 260mm (9¹/₂ x 10¹/₄in)*

# *Embroidering an outer mount*

Mounts can be painted and embroidered. Designs and three-dimensional flowers can be drawn and stitched on to the outer mount. Double mounts can be added on top to add depth. An embroidered outer mount looks particularly effective if it is a continuation of the stitched scene, or it could be a separate design altogether as long as it complements the colours and textures of the inner embroidery.

In the embroidery illustrated here, which is entitled Misty Loch, the theme is continued on to the mount. The foreground grasses and flowers mask the mount effectively and form a screen through which the lake is viewed. Two separate embroideries are worked. The inner scene is shown below. The embroidery on the opposite page forms the outer mount.

These are the most difficult mounts to put together, and you should be particularly careful when cutting the top left and right hand corners. If these corners are accidentally over cut, you can cover them up by making a few more grasses and flowers and attaching them to both edges of the outer mount. Many a mistake has resulted in a more creative embroidery!

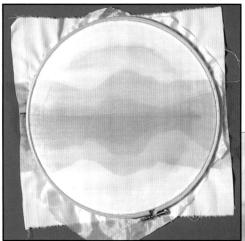

*The silk is stretched on a ring frame and the sky and lake are cut out of chiffon and trapped between the cotton background fabric and top habotai silk. The horizon line is darker than the surrounding areas, where the lake meets the sky.*

*Grasses and flowers are embroidered on to the silk using single strands of thread.*

Dense foliage and flowers are embroidered on to painted
silk. Three-dimensional leaves, grasses and flowers are
stitched on afterwards with tiny stitches.

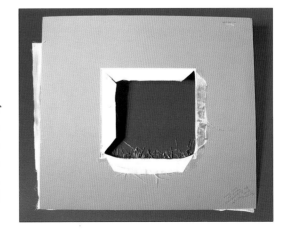

The mount is marked out and the centre rectangle of
the scene above is cut out. The embroidery is
stretched over the mount, and the back is glued to
the edges. When it is free from wrinkles, the centre
rectangle is cut out, with at least 25mm (1in) left to
turn under. The silk is cut into each corner and
glued down on the back of the mount.

## Misty Loch
BERYL DAVIDSON

*The finished embroidery.*
*235 x 315mm (9¹/₄ x 12³/₈in)*

## Norfolk Lavender Fields
KATHRYN SPENDILOW

*Like Beryl's Misty Loch, this embroidery is in two*
*parts, which adds to the strong sense of perspective.*
*Kathryn has achieved an unusual effect on the outer*
*mount by leaving out, rather than including, certain*
*stitches. This is a very precise piece of work.*

*75 x 150mm (3 x 5⁷/₈in)*

# Inspiration and interpretation

No two embroiderers will interpret a scene in the same way. Each person sees different things in the landscape. Here, one subject has been interpreted in two ways. Diane and Judy have used a variety of techniques, and although both embroideries are similar, there are obvious differences.

## Casa España

*JUDY HARGREAVES*

*Judy leaves the walls plain, but she fills in the door and windows with stitches. Silk is stretched over cut-out cardboard frames to create the window and door surrounds. The cobbles are quilted; the grape vine is made from stiffened hessian; the grapes are French knots worked on to cold water soluble fabric; and the lemons are made from oven-hardening clay (see page 70).*

*160 x 245mm (6¹/₄ x 9⁵/₈in)*

## Spanish Courtyard

### DIANE HARDING

*Diane enjoys using painted backgrounds, adding stitches to highlight or enhance certain features.
This embroidery has been built up in layers and three rings have been used – one for the blue house,
another for the rustic wall on the left which was painted, embroidered, then stretched over
mounting card, and the third for the small wall and the plant pots. The stained silk is ruched up
and held in place with multi-coloured stitches. The little garden and plant pots are filled with cold
water soluble fabric flowers and foliage. The vine is split, twisted and stiffened, and finally, little
fabric leaves and balls of stained silk are stitched on to it.*

*120 x 160mm (4³/₄ x 6¹/₄in)*

## Trellised Garden

### JEAN MILLS

*Jean stitched the distant hedge and trees first, then the path and borders. The trellis is made using fine pieces of wood, and hessian wisteria is twisted in and out of the posts. Fabric leaves and French knots worked on cold water soluble fabric are attached to the hessian. To add further interest, Jean has split her mounts and positioned a plant pot made of silk between them. Paint is stippled on to her mount and finally, another plant pot and piece of trellis have been added to complete the frame.*

*160 x 180mm (6¼ x 7⅛in)*

Here, Jean and June have chosen the same subject but, as on the previous pages, they have interpreted the scene in different ways.

Deciding what to embroider is an important part of the build up of a picture. Gardening books, magazines, parks and garden centres are a good source of inspiration. It is essential that your chosen scene contains plenty of interest. A large field of grass could be a little monotonous, but grass has its own texture and colour, and a field of different grasses, with some flowers and foliage, would make a much more interesting picture.

My students and I have spent many happy hours planning and working our pictures. I hope that you will now go on to create your own embroideries, using the techniques I have shown you in this book.

*The embroidery above can be seen in more detail on page 74 .*

# Index